To all beginners and experts stepping into the world of creativity and presentation.

May this guide empower you to craft compelling stories and impactful designs.

Your journey starts here—explore, learn, and create with confidence!

TABLE OF CONTENTS

Introduction

Microsoft Office 365 is a cloud-based productivity suite that includes a wide range of applications, including PowerPoint and Publisher. These tools are specifically designed to help users create engaging presentations and professional-quality publications, simplifying the process of communicating ideas visually and effectively. Unlike standalone desktop versions, Office 365 allows you to access these applications via the cloud, enabling you to work from anywhere, on any device with internet connectivity.

Whether you're designing stunning presentations, crafting professional newsletters, or creating customized marketing materials, PowerPoint and Publisher provide intuitive tools to bring your ideas to life. Through OneDrive, another Microsoft service, your work is securely stored in the cloud, ensuring easy access across all devices and seamless collaboration with colleagues in real time.

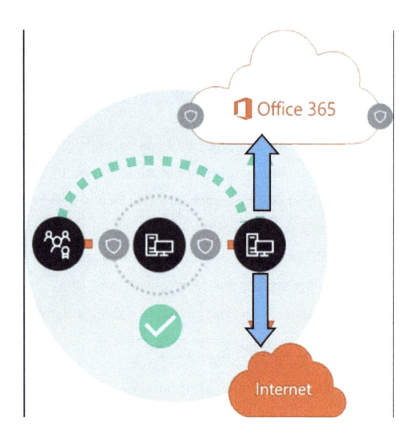

Benefits and Features of Cloud-Based Applications

Cloud-based applications like PowerPoint and Publisher in Office 365 offer several advantages:

- **Access Anytime, Anywhere**: With an internet connection, you can create, edit, and present your work from any device—be it Windows, Mac, iOS, or Android. This flexibility is invaluable for professionals and students alike.

- **Collaborative Editing**: PowerPoint allows multiple users to work on the same presentation simultaneously, making teamwork more efficient. Publisher makes it easy to share and get feedback on design projects.
- **Automatic Updates**: Office 365 ensures that you're always working with the latest features and security enhancements, with updates applied automatically.
- **Secure Cloud Storage**: Files saved to OneDrive are backed up automatically and protected against data loss, offering peace of mind and easy access whenever you need them.

Why PowerPoint and Publisher?

These tools offer unique strengths for communication and design:

- **PowerPoint for Presentations**: Create dynamic slides with animations, images, and videos to captivate your audience. Whether for business, education, or personal projects, PowerPoint makes presenting ideas straightforward and impactful.
- **Publisher for Publications**: From flyers and brochures to newsletters and postcards, Publisher provides customizable templates and powerful design tools to create polished materials that stand out.

How to Use This Book

This book is a beginner-friendly guide designed to teach you the essential features and advanced capabilities of PowerPoint and Publisher. With step-by-step instructions, helpful visuals, and practical examples, you'll gain hands-on experience as you explore both applications.

Each chapter is structured to walk you through basic features and gradually introduce more advanced tools. Whether you're new to these programs or looking to enhance your skills, this guide will help you navigate their functionalities with ease.

By the end of this book, you'll be equipped to:

- Use **PowerPoint** to create visually compelling presentations with confidence.
- Leverage **Publisher** to design professional-quality publications tailored to your needs.

So, let's get started and unlock the potential of Microsoft PowerPoint and Publisher!

Chapter 1 – Getting Started with Microsoft Office 365

Microsoft 365 is a versatile cloud-based suite that offers a wide range of productivity tools, including PowerPoint and Publisher. These applications are essential for creating professional presentations and visually appealing publications. This chapter will guide you through the steps to get started with these tools, ensuring you can harness their full potential.

Choosing the Right Microsoft 365 Subscription

Before installing Microsoft 365, it's crucial to select a subscription plan that meets your needs. Microsoft offers various options tailored for different users:

- **Personal Subscription**: Designed for individual users, this plan provides full access to Office apps, including PowerPoint and Publisher, and 1TB of OneDrive storage. Ideal for personal and light professional use.

- **Family Subscription**: Perfect for households, this plan allows up to six users, with each person receiving their own 1TB of OneDrive storage.
- **Business Subscription**: Targeted at small businesses, this plan includes Office apps, business email via Outlook, advanced collaboration tools, and heightened security features.
- **Student/Teacher Subscription**: Eligible students and educators can access Microsoft 365 Education for free, which includes PowerPoint, Publisher, OneDrive, and Teams.

Explore Microsoft's subscription options at [Microsoft's official site](https://www.microsoft.com/en-us/microsoft-365/get-started-with-office-365) at https://www.microsoft.com/en-us/microsoft-365/get-started-with-office-365 to find the plan that best fits your needs.

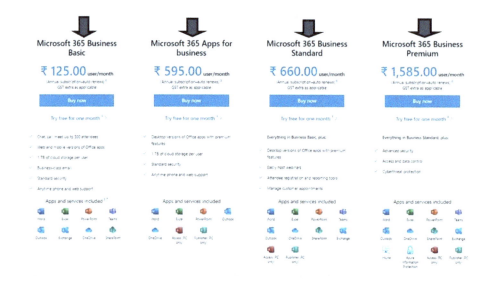

Installing Microsoft 365 for PowerPoint and Publisher

Once you've selected your subscription, follow these steps to install Microsoft 365 on different devices:

For Windows:

1. Visit the Microsoft 365 download page at [Microsoft Download](). At https://www.microsoft.com/en-us/microsoft-365/get-started-with-office-365
2. Sign in with your Microsoft account or create one.
3. Click the **Install Office** button to download the setup file.
4. Run the installer and follow the prompts to complete the installation.
5. Launch PowerPoint or Publisher and sign in with your Microsoft account to activate.

For Mac:

1. Access the Microsoft 365 download page for Mac.
2. Sign in with your Microsoft account.
3. Download the Office installer for Mac.
4. Follow the on-screen steps to install the suite.
5. Open PowerPoint or Publisher and sign in to activate your subscription.

1. Visit the App Store (iOS) or Google Play Store (Android).
2. Search for Microsoft PowerPoint or Publisher.
3. Download and install the apps.
4. Sign in with your Microsoft account to begin using them on the go.

Navigating the Microsoft 365 Dashboard

The Microsoft 365 dashboard serves as your central hub for accessing all Office apps, including PowerPoint and Publisher.

- **Homepage**: The homepage features icons for frequently used apps. You can pin PowerPoint and Publisher to the top for quick access.
- **Search Bar**: Use the search bar to locate files, apps, or collaborators.
- **Apps Menu**: Access the app launcher (the "Waffle" icon) to explore additional tools like Teams, OneDrive, and Access.
- **Settings**: Manage your account settings, notifications, and themes by clicking your profile icon in the top-right corner.

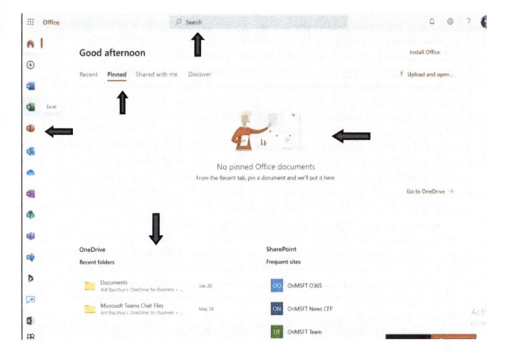

Setting Up and Personalizing Your Account

To unlock all features of Microsoft 365, you need a Microsoft account. If you don't already have one, here's how to create it:

1. Visit the Microsoft Account Signup Page. At https://signup.live.com/
2. Provide your email address or create a new one (Outlook or Hotmail).
3. Set a secure password and confirm it.
4. Verify your identity with a code sent to your email or phone.

5. Sign in to Microsoft 365 with your new account credentials.

Personalizing Your Profile:

- **Change Profile Picture**: Update your profile photo for a personalized experience by selecting **Edit Profile** under your profile icon.
- **Set Preferences**: Adjust language and region settings via **Settings > Language and Region**.
- **Enable Two-Factor Authentication**: Add an extra layer of security to your account to safeguard your data.

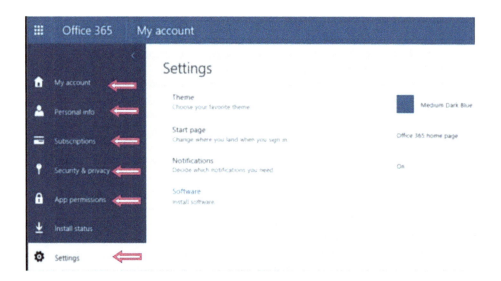

WELCOME TO GUIDE ON

MICROSOFT

POWERPOINT

Chapter 2 – Microsoft PowerPoint for Beginners

Microsoft PowerPoint is a widely used tool for creating visually engaging presentations. Whether you're giving a business pitch, teaching a class, or sharing ideas in a meeting, PowerPoint is the go-to software for building slideshows that combine text, images, videos, and animations. It's part of the Microsoft Office suite, and it's designed to help you convey information in an organized and visually appealing way.

Uses of PowerPoint presentations

- **Business Meetings**: Presenting data, ideas, and strategies clearly to clients and stakeholders.
- **Education**: Teachers and students create presentations to share information in classrooms.
- **Conferences & Seminars**: Speakers use PowerPoint to guide their discussions with visual aids.
- **Marketing & Sales**: Product demos and pitches are often accompanied by visually rich slides to captivate potential customers.

PowerPoint allows you to create dynamic and professional-looking presentations that engage your audience. Whether it's a simple presentation or a complex multimedia slideshow, PowerPoint has a wide range of tools that can be utilized to enhance your content.

Example of a Business Presentation in PowerPoint

Creating a New Presentation from Scratch or Template

1: Open PowerPoint

To start, launch Microsoft PowerPoint from your Microsoft 365 menu or from your computer. If it's not open yet, you can find it by searching for "PowerPoint" in your Start menu or Applications folder.

2: Choose a Presentation Type

When you first open PowerPoint, you'll see options to either start a presentation from scratch or use a template.

- **Blank Presentation**: This option allows you to create a presentation from scratch. You'll have a clean slate to design your slides however you like.
- **Templates**: If you want a pre-designed look, choose a template. Templates are ready-made slide designs with colors, fonts, and layouts that you can customize for your presentation.

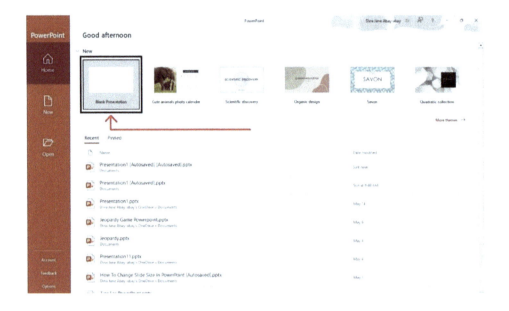

3: Starting with a Blank Presentation

If you chose "Blank Presentation," PowerPoint will open a new file with a title slide. Here's how to proceed:

- **Adding a New Slide**: To add more slides, click on the "Home" tab and select the "New Slide" button. You can choose different layouts for each slide, such as Title and Content, Two Content, or Blank, depending on the design you want.
- **Adding Text**: Click inside the text boxes on the slides to type your content. If there are no text boxes, you can click "Insert" from the top menu, then choose "Text Box" to add one.

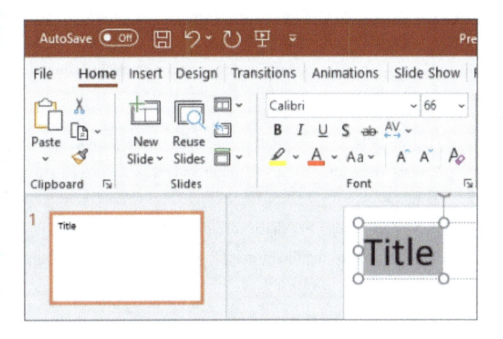

4: Starting with a Template

If you prefer to work with a template:

- **Select a Template**: When you open PowerPoint, look for the "New" tab and browse through the available templates. You can choose a specific category like Business, Education, or a Simple design.
- **Customize the Template**: Once you select a template, it will open as a presentation with pre-designed slides. You can change the text, colors, and images to fit your content.

5: Save Your Presentation

After making your slides, save your presentation to avoid losing your work:

- Click on "File" in the top-left corner, then select "Save As."
- Choose a location on your computer and give your presentation a name.
- If you're ready to share or present, select "PowerPoint Presentation" as the file format to save it in the traditional .pptx format.

8: Start Presenting

To present your slides, click the "Slide Show" tab and select "From Beginning" to start the presentation from the first slide. You can also press the "F5" key to start the presentation quickly.

Navigating the PowerPoint Interface

Understanding the Ribbon, Slides Pane, and the Slide Sorter View

1. **The Ribbon**:
   - The **Ribbon** is the main toolbar in PowerPoint, located at the top of the window. It contains various tabs, such as

Home, **Insert**, **Design**, **Transitions**, **Animations**, and **Slide Show**, each grouping together related tools.

- For example, the **Home** tab includes essential tools like **Font Formatting**, **Paragraph** tools, and **New Slide**. Each tab gives you access to tools and commands that will help you design your presentation.

2. **Slides Pane**:

   - On the left side of the screen, you'll see the **Slides Pane**. This pane shows thumbnails of your slides, allowing you to quickly navigate between slides in your presentation. It also enables you to reorder slides by dragging and dropping them.

   - The **Slide Sorter View** can be activated by selecting **View > Slide Sorter** from the Ribbon. This view allows you to see all your slides at once and rearrange them more easily.

3. **Slide Area**:

   - The central area of the PowerPoint window is where you design individual slides. This area allows you to add text, images, shapes, and more. It's where you will spend most of your time while working on your presentation.

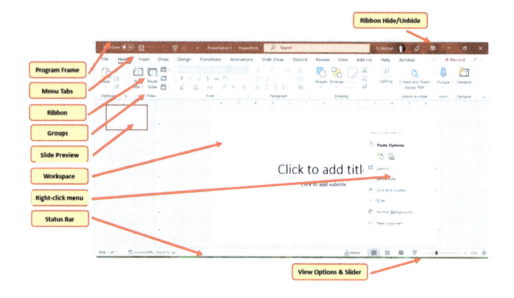

Creating and Formatting Slides

Adding Text, Images, and Shapes to Slides

1. **Adding Text**:
   - Open your PowerPoint presentation and go to the slide where you want to add text.
   - Click on the text box placeholder that says "Click to add text." If there is no placeholder, click on the "Insert" tab at the top, and then click on "Text Box."
   - Click anywhere on the slide where you want to place the text box. A box will appear.

- Start typing your text. You can adjust the font, size, and color using the options in the "Home" tab under the "Font" section.
- If you need to move the text box, click on the text box border and drag it to a new location.

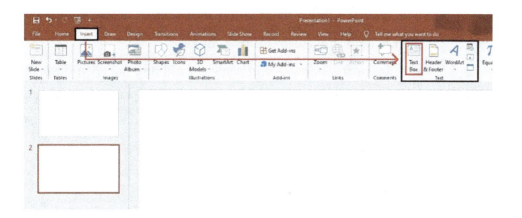

2. **Adding Images**:
- Go to the slide where you want to insert an image.
- Click on the "Insert" tab at the top of PowerPoint.
- Click on the "Pictures" button. You can choose to add a picture from your computer by selecting "This Device," or you can insert an online image by selecting "Online Pictures."

- If you choose "This Device," browse to the location of the image on your computer, click the image you want, and then click "Insert."
- The image will appear on your slide. Resize it by clicking and dragging the corners. You can also move it by clicking and dragging the image to a different spot.

3. **Adding Shapes**:
    - Go to the slide where you want to insert a shape.
    - Click on the "Insert" tab at the top.
    - Click on "Shapes," and a menu will appear with different types of shapes like rectangles, circles, arrows, and more.

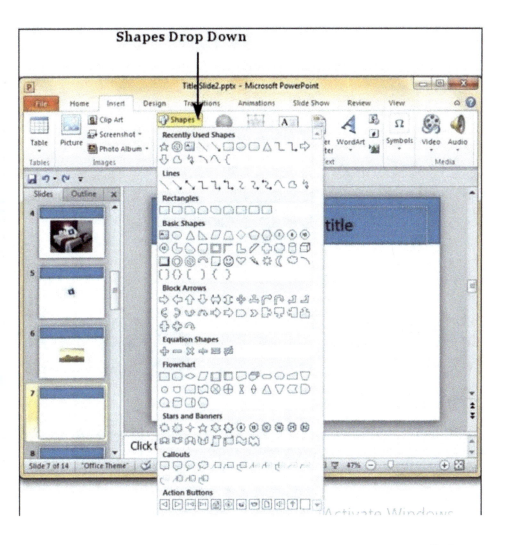

- Click on the shape you want to use. Your cursor will change to a crosshair.
- Click and drag on the slide to draw the shape. You can adjust its size by dragging the corners or sides.

- After adding the shape, you can change its color, border, or effects by using the "Format" tab.

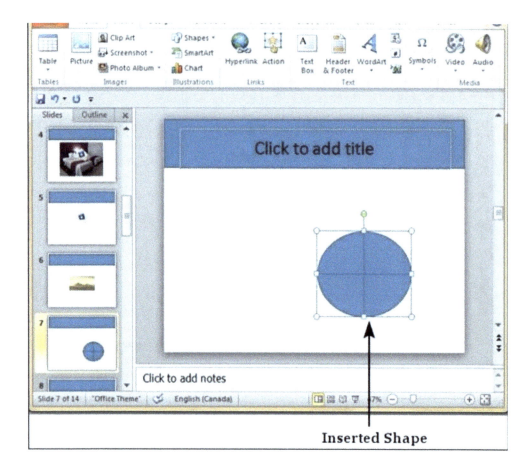

Inserted Shape

Using Bullet Points, Numbering, and Slide Layouts

Bullet points and numbering in PowerPoint are essential tools for organizing and presenting information clearly and effectively. Here's an overview of their uses and functions:

Uses of Bullet Points in PowerPoint

1. **Breaking Down Information**: Bullet points simplify complex topics into smaller, digestible chunks, making it easier for the audience to follow.
2. **Highlighting Key Points**: They draw attention to the most important information in a slide, ensuring the audience remembers the critical details.
3. **Improving Readability**: Bullet points create a visual separation between ideas, making content less overwhelming and more visually appealing.
4. **Encouraging Focus**: By limiting the amount of text on a slide, bullet points help keep the audience's attention on your speech or visuals.
5. **Supporting Visual Flow**: They guide the viewer's eye through the content in a structured manner.

Uses of Numbering in PowerPoint

1. **Presenting Sequential Steps**: Numbering is ideal for showing processes, instructions, or chronological events in a clear, step-by-step format.
2. **Organizing Priorities**: Numbered lists can rank information by importance, helping the audience understand the hierarchy or order of ideas.
3. **Simplifying Complex Concepts**: Like bullet points, numbering breaks down complex ideas, but with an added sense of order or sequence.
4. **Encouraging Structured Discussion**: It helps presenters and audiences refer to specific points during discussions, making communication more efficient.

Functions of Bullet Points and Numbering

1. **Clarity and Conciseness**: Both tools condense lengthy explanations into concise phrases, aiding quick comprehension.
2. **Enhancing Slide Design**: Bullet points and numbering improve the slide layout by adding structure and reducing text clutter.
3. **Visual Impact**: They create a clean, professional appearance that enhances the overall presentation quality.

4. **Support for Visual Memory**: Audiences often remember ideas better when they are grouped or ordered visually using bullets or numbers.

The following is a step-by-step guide on how to insert Bullet Points and Numbering in a PowerPoint presentation:

1. **Bullet Points**:
    -   **Select the Text Box**: First, click on the text box where you want to add your bullet points. If there's no text box, click "Insert" in the top menu, then choose "Text Box" to add one.
    -   **Choose the Bullet Points**: Highlight the text you want to turn into a list. On the Home tab, in the Paragraph group, you'll see the Bullet Points icon (a dot with lines). Click it to turn your text into bullets.

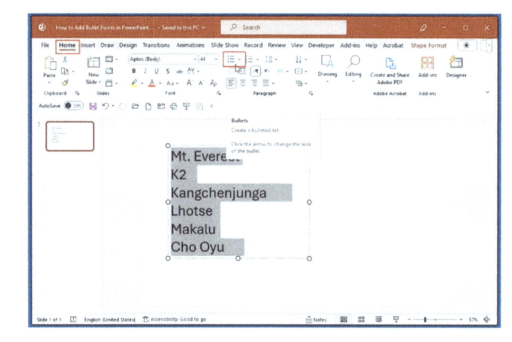

- **Customize the Bullets**: You can customize the bullets by clicking the small arrow next to the Bullet Points icon. Here, you can select different symbols or even use your own image as a bullet point.

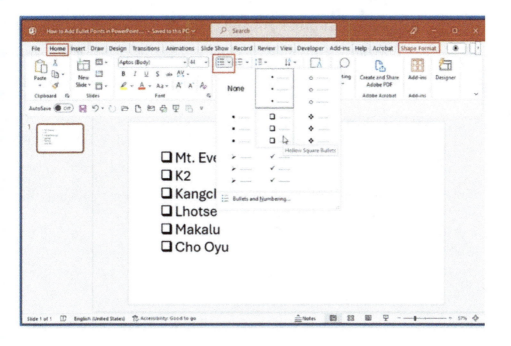

- **Adjust Bullet Style**: To change the size, color, or alignment of the bullet points, select the text, right-click, and choose "Bullets and Numbering." This will give you more options for customization.

2. **Using Numbering**:

- **Highlight the Text**: Select the lines of text where you want to use numbering.
- **Apply Numbering**: On the Home tab, look for the Numbering icon (a set of numbers with lines). Click it, and your selected text will turn into a numbered list.

- **Choose Number Format**: Just like bullet points, you can change the numbering style. Click the small arrow next to the Numbering icon to pick from a variety of styles, like numbers, letters, or Roman numerals.
- **Adjust the Numbering Style**: To change how the numbers appear, right-click the numbered list and choose "Numbering and Bullets" to explore more settings, like changing the starting number.

3. **Slide Layouts**:

Slide layouts in Microsoft PowerPoint are pre-designed templates that determine the structure and arrangement of content on a slide. They are essential for creating organized, consistent, and visually appealing presentations.

Uses of Slide Layouts

1. **Consistency Across Slides**: Slide layouts ensure that all slides in your presentation maintain a uniform structure and design, making it easier for your audience to follow.
2. **Ease of Design**: Layouts provide a starting point, so you don't need to manually arrange text boxes, images, or other elements whenever you create a new slide.
3. **Time-saving**: By selecting a layout that fits your needs, you can quickly add content without worrying about formatting.
4. **Professional Appearance**: Pre-designed layouts help your presentation look polished and professional with minimal effort.
5. **Accessibility**: Layouts are designed with accessibility in mind, ensuring elements like headings and text are arranged for readability.

Functions of Slide Layouts

1. **Placement of Content**: Layouts dictate where placeholders for text, images, charts, videos, or other elements will appear on a slide.
   - For example, the **Title Slide** layout positions a large heading at the top and a subtitle below it.

2. **Guiding Content Structure**: Each layout serves a specific purpose:
   - **Title and Content**: Ideal for adding a slide title with a list, image, or chart.
   - **Comparison**: Best for comparing two sets of information side by side.
   - **Picture with Caption**: Allows you to display an image with a caption beneath it.

3. **Customization Options**: While layouts provide a default structure, they are flexible. You can add, move, or resize elements within the layout to suit your needs.

4. **Integration with Slide Master**: Slide layouts are linked to the Slide Master, which controls the overall design (such as fonts, colors, and background) for all slides in a presentation.

5. **Automatic Formatting**: When you select a layout, PowerPoint automatically applies the associated formatting, including font sizes, styles, and alignment.

Examples of Common Slide Layouts

1. **Title Slide**: For introductory slides, containing a title and subtitle placeholder.

2. **Title and Content**: For slides with a heading and either text or multimedia content.

3. **Section Header**: Marks the beginning of a new section in your presentation.

4. **Two Content**: Displays two placeholders for text or objects side by side.

5. **Blank**: No placeholders; perfect for creating custom layouts from scratch.

Below is a step by step guide on how to insert slide layouts in PowerPoint:

- **Insert a New Slide**: Go to the Home tab, then click "New Slide." A small menu will appear with different layout options like Title Slide, Title and Content, Comparison, etc.

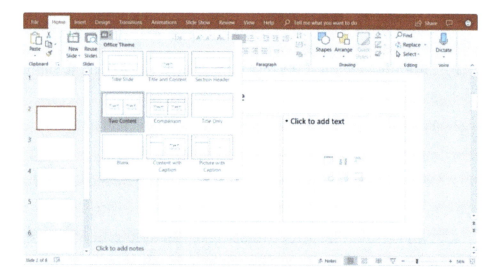

- **Choose the Layout**: Each slide layout serves a different purpose. For example:
  - **Title Slide**: For your presentation's introduction.
  - **Title and Content**: Perfect for adding headings and bullet points.
  - **Comparison**: Best for comparing two items side by side.
  - **Blank**: No placeholders, ideal for creating custom layouts.
- **Customize Your Layout**: After inserting a layout, you can add or remove placeholders like text boxes, images, and charts by clicking and dragging them. You can also resize or reposition any elements on the slide.

- **Change Layouts on Existing Slides**: If you want to change the layout of an already existing slide, right-click the slide thumbnail on the left, choose "Layout," and select the new layout style you prefer.

Designing Presentations

Applying and Customizing Themes

PowerPoint themes are a quick way to give your presentation a polished and consistent look. They include preset combinations of colors, fonts, and background styles. Here's how you can apply and customize themes:

1. Navigate to the Design Tab
   - On the PowerPoint ribbon at the top of your screen, click the **Design** tab.
   - This tab contains all the tools you need to apply and customize themes.

2. Apply a Theme
   - In the **Themes** group, you'll see several thumbnails of available themes. Hover your cursor over each one to preview how it would look on your slides.
   - Once you find a theme you like, click on it to apply it to your presentation.
   - The theme will automatically update all your slides with the new design.
3. Customize the Theme Colors
   - To tweak the colors, click on the **More** button in the **Variants** group (it's a small down-arrow icon).

   - Select **Colors** > **Customize Colors** from the dropdown menu.
   - In the dialog box, you can assign custom colors to different elements, such as text, background, or hyperlinks.
   - Name your new color scheme and click **Save** to apply it.

4. Modify the Fonts
   - In the **More** button under the **Variants** section, select **Fonts > Customize Fonts**.
   - In the font customization window, choose the font styles for the headings and body text.
   - Give your new font set a name and click **Save** to apply the changes.
5. Adjust the Background Style
   - To change the slide background, go to the **Background** group in the **Design** tab.
   - Click **Format Background**, which opens a pane on the right.
   - Choose from options like **Solid Fill**, **Gradient Fill**, or **Picture or Texture Fill** to customize the background.
   - Once satisfied, click **Apply to All** to use the new background on every slide, or leave it applied to a single slide.

Working with Master Slides for Consistent Design

Master Slide is like a blueprint for your presentation. It controls the appearance of all the slides, including fonts, colors, backgrounds, and layouts. When you edit a Master Slide, the changes automatically apply to every related slide in your presentation.

1. Access the Slide Master

    - Open your PowerPoint presentation.

    - Click on the **View** tab in the top menu.

    - Select **Slide Master** from the ribbon. This will take you to
      a new view showing the Master Slide and its layouts on the
      left-hand side.

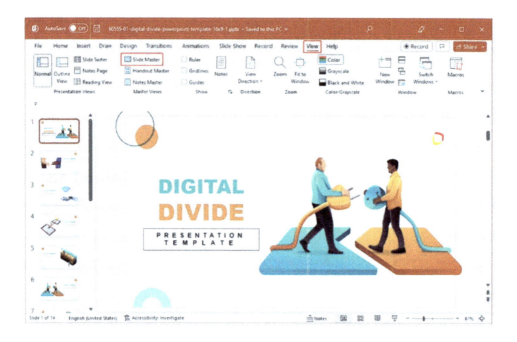

2. Edit the Master Slide

    - The first, larger slide at the top of the panel is the Master
      Slide. Any changes you make here will affect all the slides
      in your presentation.

- For example, to change the background, click **Background Styles** and select a new style or color.
- You can also update the font style by selecting the text and using the formatting options in the **Home** tab.

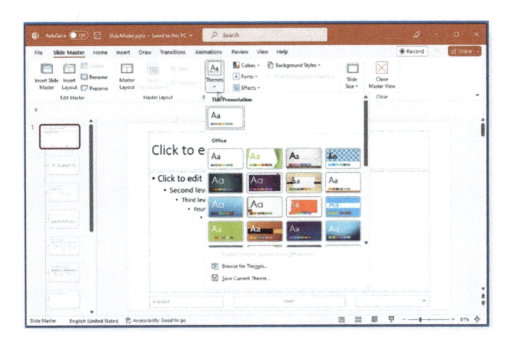

3. Customize Layouts

- Below the Master Slide, you'll see smaller slides called **Layout Slides**. These are individual templates for specific slide types (e.g., title slide, content slide).
- Click on a Layout Slide to customize it. For example, you can add placeholders for text, images, or charts to create a consistent layout.

4. Apply Themes for a Cohesive Look
   - On the **Slide Master** tab, select **Themes** to choose a pre-designed style that fits your presentation.
   - Themes adjust colors, fonts, and effects to ensure your slides look polished and unified.
5. Save Time with Custom Placeholders
   - To make it easy to add content later, you can create placeholders on the Layout Slides.
   - Click **Insert Placeholder** on the Slide Master toolbar, then choose the type of content you want (text, image, chart, etc.).
   - Position the placeholder where you want it on the slide.
6. Close the Master View
   - Once you've finished customizing your Master Slides, click **Close Master View** in the ribbon. You'll return to the normal editing view of your presentation.
   - Now, all slides in your presentation will automatically reflect the changes you made in the Master Slide.
7. Apply a Layout to a Slide
   - When creating a new slide, go to the **Home** tab and click **Layout**.
   - Choose a layout from the list that matches the design you set up in the Slide Master.
8. Update the Master Slide Later

- If you need to make further adjustments, simply return to the **Slide Master** view and make your changes.
- Remember, any updates you make will apply instantly to all the linked slides, saving you time.

9. Save Your Customized Theme
   - To reuse your design for other presentations, save your customized theme.
   - Go to the **Design** tab, click the drop-down arrow in the Themes section, and choose **Save Current Theme**. Give it a name and save it for future use.

Using SmartArt and Icons for Visual Appeal

1. Open Your PowerPoint Slide
   - Start PowerPoint and open your presentation.
   - Choose the slide where you want to add SmartArt or icons. This could be a title slide, content slide, or any slide needing visual enhancement.

2. Access the SmartArt Tool
   - Go to the **Insert** tab on the ribbon at the top of the screen.
   - Click on **SmartArt** in the "Illustrations" group. This opens a dialog box displaying different SmartArt options.

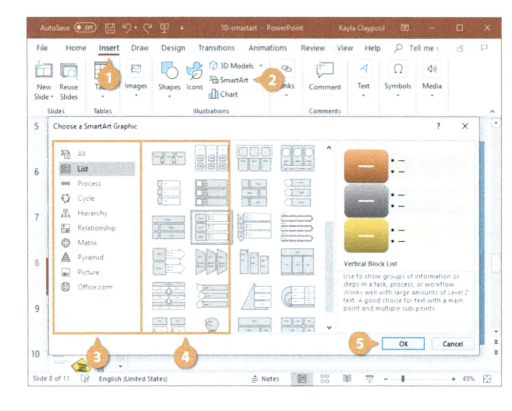

3. Select a SmartArt Graphic

    - Browse the categories such as **List**, **Process**, **Cycle**, or **Hierarchy**. Each category organizes information differently.

    - Click on a style that suits your content. For example: Use **List** for bullet points. Choose **Process** for step-by-step instructions.

    - Once you've made your selection, click **OK** to insert it into your slide.

SmartArt Graphic Types	
List	Show non-sequential information.
Process	Show steps in a process or timeline.
Cycle	Show a continual process.
Hierarchy	Create an organization chart or decision tree.
Relationship	Illustrate connections.
Matrix	Show how parts relate to a whole.
Pyramid	Show proportional relationships with the largest component on the top or bottom.
Picture	Create a SmartArt graphic that incorporates pictures.

4. Add Text to SmartArt

- Click inside the boxes or placeholders in the SmartArt graphic.
- Type your text directly. For instance, if you're creating a process chart, write each step in the appropriate box.
- Use the text pane on the left (if visible) for easier editing. If it's not showing, click the small arrow on the left side of the SmartArt to open it.

1 Select the SmartArt Diagram.

2 Click the arrow at the left edge of the SmartArt graphic.

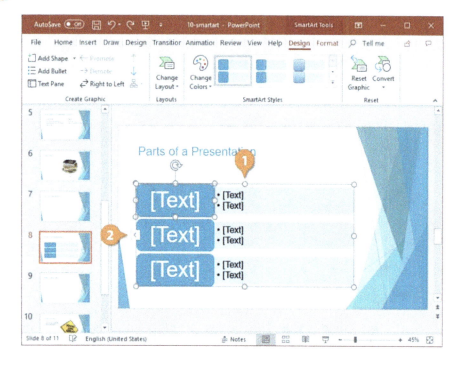

5. Customize the SmartArt Design

- With the SmartArt selected, go to the **SmartArt Design** tab that appears on the ribbon.
- Use the options in the "Styles" group to change the appearance: **Change Colors** - Pick a color scheme that matches your slide theme. **SmartArt Styles** - Apply effects like 3D, shadows, or outlines to make it more attractive.

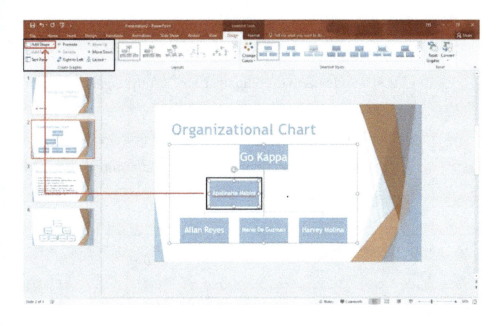

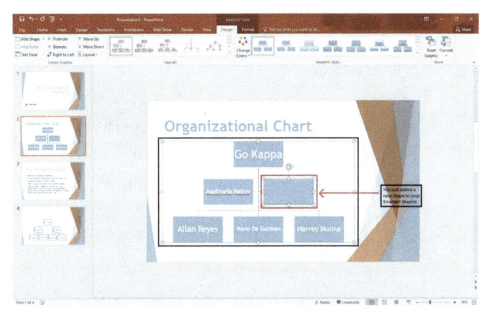

6. Insert Icons

- Go back to the **Insert** tab.
- Click on **Icons** in the "Illustrations" group. A gallery of icons will appear.
- Use the search bar to find specific icons. For example, type "arrow" for directional icons or "computer" for tech-related visuals.

7. Add Icons to the Slide

- Select one or more icons by clicking on them.
- Click the **Insert** button to place the icons on your slide.
- Resize or move the icons by dragging the corners or edges. Position them to complement your content.

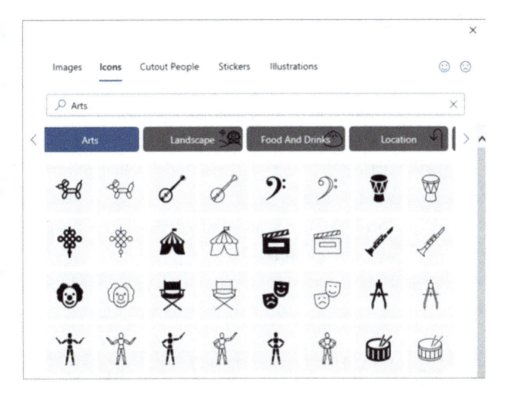

8. Customize Icons

    - With the icon selected, go to the **Graphics Format** tab on the ribbon.

    - Change the **color** to match your slide design. You can pick from preset theme colors or customize your own.

    - Adjust the icon's **size** and **position** to fit neatly with your text or SmartArt.

9. Combine SmartArt and Icons

- Use icons alongside your SmartArt to add extra meaning. For instance: Add a gear icon next to a step that involves "settings." Place a lightbulb icon near ideas or solutions.
- Ensure the visuals are balanced and don't overcrowd the slide.

10. Preview and Finalize

- Click **Slide Show** to preview how your SmartArt and icons look during a presentation.
- Make any final adjustments to alignment, size, or colors.
- Save your presentation to preserve the changes.

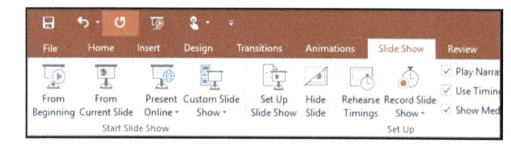

Advanced Features in PowerPoint

Adding Transitions and Animations

Transitions are effects applied when moving from one slide to another, while animations are effects added to individual elements on a slide, such as text, images, or shapes.

Adding Transitions between Slides

- Select a Slide: Click on the slide thumbnail in the left panel where you want to add a transition.

- Go to the Transitions Tab: On the top menu bar, click the **Transitions** tab.

- Choose a Transition Effect: Browse through the available effects like **Fade**, **Wipe**, or **Morph** in the **Transition to This Slide** group. Click on an effect to apply it to the selected slide.

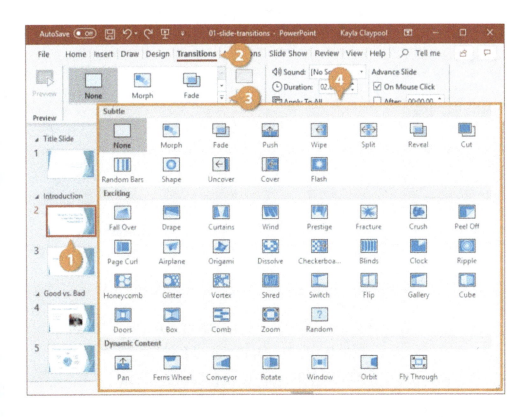

- Customize Transition Options: Adjust its settings in the Effect Options dropdown after choosing a transition. For example: Change the direction of the transition (e.g., left to right or top to bottom). Adjust the duration using the **Duration** box to make the transition faster or slower.

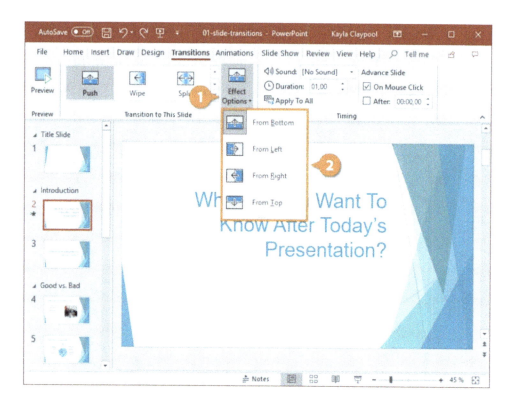

- Apply to All Slides (Optional): To apply the same transition to every slide, click **Apply To All** in the ribbon.
- Preview the Transition: Click **Preview** to see how the transition looks.

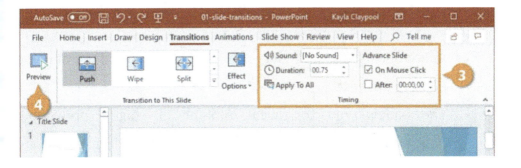

Adding Animations to Slide Elements

Adding animations in PowerPoint can significantly enhance your presentation by making it more engaging, professional, and effective. Below are the key benefits of using animations in your slides:

1. Captures Attention

- Animations help draw the audience's focus to specific parts of the slide, ensuring important content stands out.
- Dynamic movement can prevent monotony and maintain interest throughout the presentation.

2. Enhances Visual Appeal

- Well-chosen animations make your slides visually appealing, creating a polished and professional look.
- Movement and effects can add a sense of creativity and modernity to your presentation.

3. Improves Content Flow

- Animations guide the audience's attention logically from one point to the next.
- They allow you to reveal content in stages, preventing information overload and keeping the audience focused on one element at a time.

4. Supports Better Understanding

- Animations can visually demonstrate processes, relationships, or changes, making complex concepts easier to understand.
- For example, using animations to show step-by-step instructions or cause-and-effect relationships enhances clarity.

5. Adds Emphasis

- Highlight specific words, images, or charts with animations to emphasize their importance.
- This helps reinforce key points and ensures they leave a lasting impression on the audience.

6. Encourages Interactivity

- Adding trigger-based animations (e.g., elements appearing when clicked) creates an interactive experience.

- This is particularly useful in training sessions, quizzes, or educational presentations.

7. Creates a Storytelling Effect

- Animations help convey a narrative by gradually building up content, much like storytelling.
- They add dramatic effect and keep the audience intrigued about what's coming next.

8. Enhances Professionalism

- When used appropriately, animations demonstrate effort and thoughtfulness in presentation design, making you appear more professional and prepared.

9. Manages Time Effectively

- Animations control the pacing of your presentation, allowing you to time discussions or explanations with the appearance of new content.

10. Keeps the Audience Engaged

- Engaging visuals paired with animations make it easier to hold the audience's attention, particularly during long presentations.

- This is especially effective in keeping younger or less attentive audiences interested.

While animations can enhance a presentation, overusing them or using distracting effects may have the opposite effect. Stick to simple, consistent animations that complement your message.

Let us now consider a step-by-step guide to using animation in your presentation:

- Select an Element to Animate: Click on the object you want to animate, such as a text box, image, or chart.
- Go to the Animations Tab: Navigate to the **Animations** tab in the top menu.

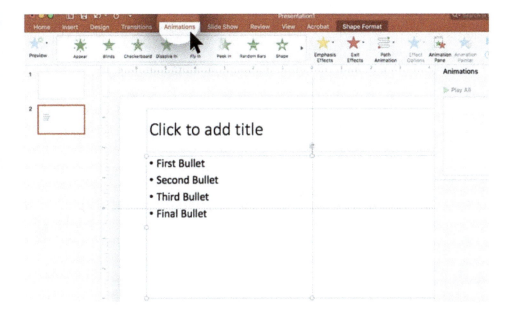

- Choose an Animation Effect: Select an animation style from the **Animation** gallery, such as: **Entrance effects** like **Fly In** or **Zoom** (to make elements appear). **Emphasis effects** like **Spin** or **Pulse** (to draw attention). **Exit effects** like **Fade Out** or **Shrink** (to make elements disappear).

- Adjust the Animation Order: If you're animating multiple elements, open the **Animation Pane** to adjust their order. Drag items up or down in the list to rearrange the sequence.

- Set Timing and Triggers: In the **Timing** group, you can: Choose when the animation starts (**On Click**, **With Previous**, or **After Previous**), adjust the duration to control how fast the animation plays, and Set delays if needed.

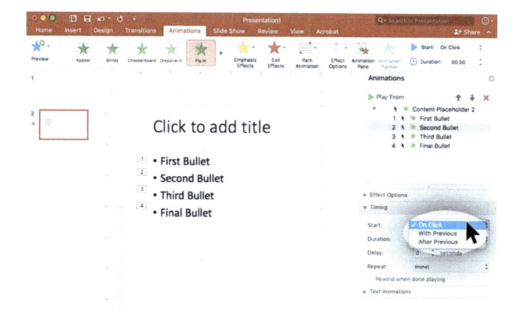

- Preview the Animation: Click **Play All** in the **Animation Pane** to see how all animations flow together on the slide.

Incorporating Audio and Video into Slides

1. Open Your Presentation: Open the presentation where you want to add audio or video. If starting fresh, create a new slide by clicking **New Slide** under the **Home** tab.
2. Select the Slide: Navigate through your presentation to find the slide where the audio or video should go. Click on the slide to select it.
3. Insert Audio: Go to the **Insert** tab in the top menu bar.

- Look for the **Audio** option in the **Media** group, usually on the far-right side.

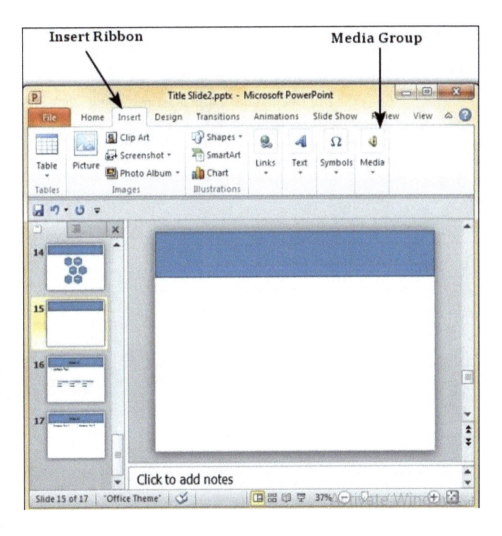

- Click the drop-down arrow under **Audio**, and choose one of the following: **Audio on My PC**: Select this if you already have an audio file saved on your computer. **Record Audio**: Choose this to record directly using your microphone.

- If you're using an audio file from your computer: Browse your files, select the audio, and click **Insert**.
- If you're recording: Name your recording in the dialog box. Click the red **Record** button to start recording. Click **Stop** when done and then **OK** to insert the recording into the slide.

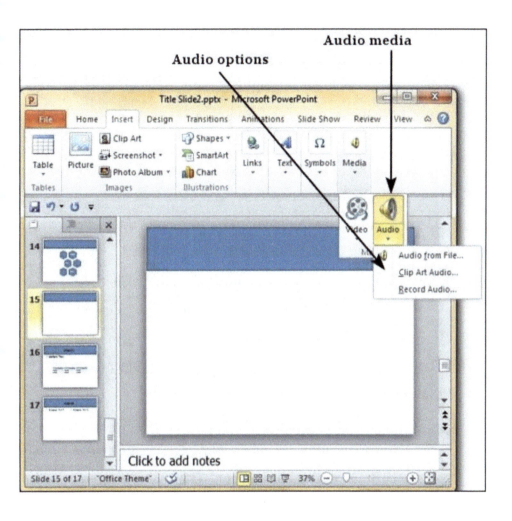

4. Insert Video: In the same **Insert** tab, locate the **Video** option, also in the **Media** group.

    • Click the drop-down arrow under **Video** and choose one of these: **Video on My PC**: For video files already saved on your device. **Online Video**: If you want to embed a video from the web.

- For a video file on your computer: Select the file, then click **Insert**.
- For an online video: Enter the URL of the video or search for one (if supported by your version of PowerPoint), then click **Insert**.

5. Position and Resize the Media: After inserting the audio or video, you'll see it on your slide as an icon or a player.
   - Drag the corners of the media box to resize it.
   - Click and drag the box to move it to your desired position on the slide.

6. Playback Options: Select the audio or video object to display the **Playback** tab in the ribbon.
   - Use the options here to customize how the media behaves: **Start**: Decide if the media plays automatically, on a mouse click, or in the background. **Trim**: Shorten the media by trimming unwanted parts. **Volume**: Adjust the playback volume. **Loop**: Set the media to replay continuously.

7. Add Controls (Optional): You can display playback controls for the video or audio. Ensure the checkbox for **Show Media Controls** is enabled in the **Playback** tab.

8. Preview Your Slide: Click **Play** on the media player to test the audio or video. Ensure the media plays as expected, and adjust settings if needed.

9. Save Your Presentation: Once you're satisfied, save your presentation by clicking **File > Save As**. Choose a location, name your file, and save it in your preferred format.

10. Test the Presentation: Start the slide show by clicking **Slide Show > From Beginning** or **From Current Slide**. Ensure the audio and video play smoothly during the presentation.

Presenting and Sharing Your Presentation

Slideshow Setup, Speaker Notes, and Presenter Tools

Setting Up Your Slideshow

1 Open Your Presentation

- Launch PowerPoint and open the file you want to present.
- Ensure all your slides are organized in the correct order.

2 Access the Slideshow Tab

- Click on the **Slideshow** tab located in the ribbon at the top of the PowerPoint window.

- This tab contains tools and options for customizing your presentation's display.

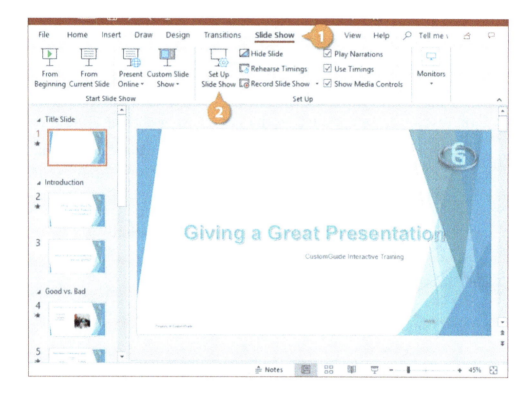

3 Configure Slideshow Settings

- In the **Set Up** group, click **Set Up Slideshow** to open a dialog box.
- Choose how the slideshow will run:
  - Presented by a speaker (full screen): Ideal for in-person presentations.

- Browsed by an individual (window): Suitable for self-paced viewing.
- Browsed at a kiosk (full screen): Best for unattended presentations, such as those at trade shows.

4 Select Slide Options

- Use checkboxes to:
  - Loop the slideshow continuously.
  - Show slides with or without narration and animation.
- Click **OK** to save your settings.

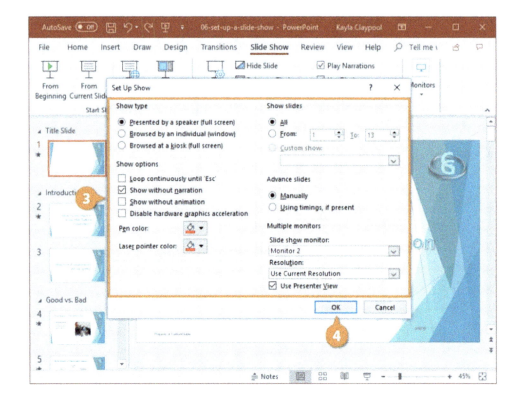

Adding and Using Speaker Notes

1 What Are Speaker Notes?

- Speaker notes are personal prompts that only you can see while
  presenting. They help you remember key points without
  crowding the slides.

2 Add Speaker Notes

- At the bottom of your PowerPoint window, locate the **Notes** section.
    - If you don't see it, click on **Notes** at the bottom-right corner to display it.
- Click inside the **Notes** pane and type your notes for the selected slide.

3 Edit and Format Notes

- Use text formatting tools in the ribbon to bold, italicize, or adjust the size of your notes for better readability.

4 View Speaker Notes

- During your presentation, you can see the notes on your device screen while your audience only sees the slides.

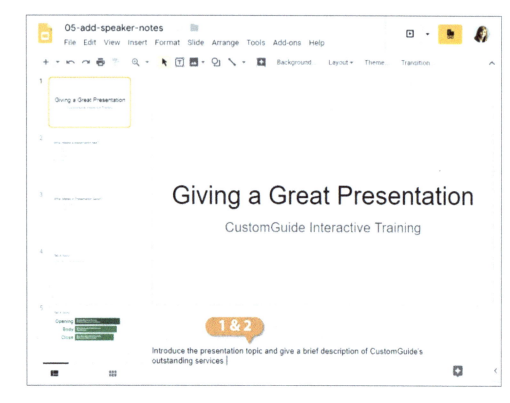

Using Presenter Tools

1. Start the Slideshow in Presenter View

- Click the **From Beginning** or **From Current Slide** option in the **Slideshow** tab to start your presentation.
- For Presenter View:
  - If it doesn't activate automatically, click **Use Presenter View** in the Slideshow settings.

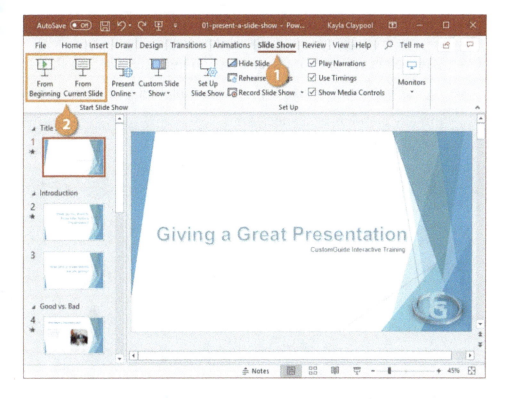

2. Understanding Presenter View Layout

- Current Slide: Displays the slide your audience is seeing.
- Next Slide Preview: Shows a thumbnail of the upcoming slide to help you prepare.
- Speaker Notes Pane: Your notes for the current slide appear here.
- Timer and Controls:
  - A timer tracks how long you've been presenting.
  - Navigation buttons allow you to move forward, backward, or jump to a specific slide.

3. Navigating During the Presentation

- Use the **arrow keys** or the **navigation buttons** to switch slides.
- If your presentation has hyperlinks or interactive elements, click directly on them as needed.

4. Tools for Engagement

- Laser Pointer, Pen, and Highlighter:
    - Move your mouse to the bottom-left corner and click on the pen icon to select a tool.
    - These tools let you emphasize parts of a slide.

- Zoom Feature:
  - Click on the magnifying glass icon to zoom in on specific slide content.

Practice Before Presenting

- Rehearse your slideshow by clicking **Rehearse Timings** in the Slideshow tab. This helps you get comfortable with transitions and timing.
- Ensure all your speaker notes are concise and aligned with the flow of your presentation.

Saving and Sharing Presentations via OneDrive

1. **Saving to OneDrive**:
   - To save your presentation to OneDrive, click on **File > Save As > OneDrive**. This will allow you to access your presentation from any device with internet access.
2. **Sharing Your Presentation**:
   - To share your presentation, go to **File > Share** and choose from options like **Email, Link,** or **Embed**. You can also collaborate in real-time with others if the file is stored on OneDrive.

WELCOME TO GUIDE ON

MICROSOFT

PUBLISHER

Chapter 3: Microsoft Publisher for Beginners

Microsoft Publisher is a desktop publishing software that is part of the Microsoft 365 suite, designed to help you create professional-quality documents, from newsletters and brochures to business cards and flyers. Unlike Microsoft Word, which is primarily used for text-based documents, Publisher is specifically focused on creating visually appealing layouts that combine text and images for a variety of print and digital formats. It provides powerful tools to help users produce marketing materials, presentations, and newsletters that are visually striking and easy to read.

In the context of Office 365, Publisher integrates well with other Microsoft applications, including Word, Excel, and PowerPoint, allowing you to import content from those programs. You can also link your Publisher designs to data sources, making it an ideal tool for creating customized documents such as mail merges or personalized invitations.

Publisher's role in Office 365 is invaluable for anyone in marketing, design, or communications. It allows users to create print-ready publications and digital files with minimal effort, even for those who may not have professional graphic design experience. Whether you're creating an invitation for a wedding, a promotional flyer for your business, or a brochure for an event, Microsoft Publisher makes it easy to bring your vision to life.

Overview of the Publisher Workspace and Tools

When you first open Microsoft Publisher, you'll be presented with the main workspace, which consists of several key areas designed to help you easily create and format your publication.

1. **Ribbon**: The **Ribbon** is the horizontal toolbar at the top of the screen that organizes all Publisher's features into tabs such as **Home**, **Insert**, **Page Design**, and **Mailings**. Each tab contains groups of related tools, such as text formatting, page layout adjustments, and design elements. This is where you'll find most of the tools you'll need for your publication.

2. **Page**: The **Page** area is the main part of the workspace where you'll design your publication. It resembles a blank sheet of paper, and you can click to add text, images, and other elements. This is where all your creative work will be displayed.

3. **Task Pane**: The **Task Pane** is a vertical panel on the right side of the screen. Here, you can access tools related to your publication's design, such as page layouts, color schemes, and font styles. It's

also where you'll find your templates, themes, and other settings to customize your publication.

4. **Navigation Pane**: The **Navigation Pane** (usually on the left side) allows you to move between multiple pages in your document, which is useful if your publication consists of more than one page. It helps you organize your publication and switch quickly between pages.

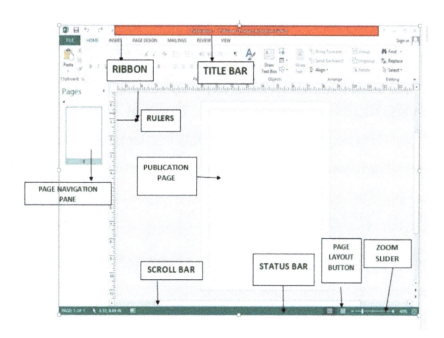

Creating Publications

Starting with a Template or Blank Page

One of the first decisions you'll need to make when creating a publication in Microsoft Publisher is whether to start from scratch with a blank page or to use a pre-designed template. Templates are a great way to jump-start your design, especially if you're unfamiliar with design principles or short on time.

1. Open Microsoft Publisher

    1. Launch Microsoft Publisher on your computer.
        - If it's your first time using Publisher, look for its icon in the Start menu or on your desktop. Click it to open.

2. Explore the Home Screen

    1. Once Publisher is open, you'll see a welcome screen. This is where you can choose how to start your project.
    2. The screen offers two main options:
        - **Templates**: Pre-designed layouts for common projects like brochures, flyers, or business cards.
        - **Blank Page**: An empty canvas for creating your design from scratch.

3. Choose a Template (Optional)

1. If you want to use a template:
   - Look at the **template categories** (e.g., Newsletters, Invitations, or Posters). These are often listed on the left side or displayed as thumbnails.
   - Click on a category to see the available designs.
   - Select a design you like by clicking on it.
2. Once you select a template:
   - You'll see a preview on the right side of the screen.
   - Adjust the template settings (e.g., size, color scheme) if options are available.
   - Click the **Create** button to open the template.

4. Start with a Blank Page (Optional)

   1. If you prefer a blank page:
      - Look for the option labeled **Blank Page Sizes** or a plain white box labeled **Blank A4** or **Blank Letter** (depending on your region).
      - Choose the size that matches your needs (e.g., 8.5 x 11 inches for standard pages).
      - Click to open a blank canvas.

5. Familiarize Yourself with the Workspace

   1. Whether you chose a template or a blank page, the main workspace will now appear.
   2. Take a moment to explore:
      - The **ribbon menu** at the top (includes tools for adding text, images, shapes, etc.).
      - The **page navigation pane** on the left (shows thumbnails of your pages if your project has multiple).
      - The **main canvas** in the center (where you'll create and edit your design).

Adding Text Boxes, Images, and Shapes to Your Publication

Once you've chosen a template or blank page, it's time to start adding content to your publication. Microsoft Publisher offers an easy way to insert text, images, and shapes, which are the core building blocks of your design.

1. Adding Text Boxes

Text boxes allow you to add and control text placement on your pages. Here's how to insert one:

1. **Open Your Publication**
   - Launch Microsoft Publisher and open the publication you're working on or start a new one.
2. **Locate the 'Text Box' Tool**
   - Go to the **Insert** tab on the Ribbon.
   - Click on **Draw Text Box** in the Text group.

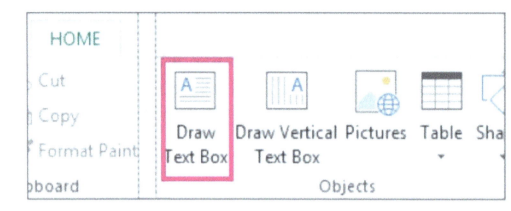

3. **Draw Your Text Box**

- Your cursor will change into a crosshair.
- Click and drag on your page where you want the text box to appear.

4. **Type Your Text**

- Click inside the text box and start typing.
- You can adjust the font, size, and color using the **Home** tab.

5. **Resize or Move the Text Box**

- To resize, click and drag the edges or corners of the box.
- To move, click inside the box and drag it to the desired location.

When a text box has too much text, a little box with ellipses appears in the lower right of the text box.

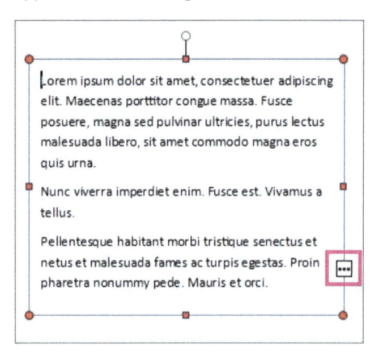

2. Adding Images

Images enhance the visual appeal of your publication. Here's how to insert them:

1. **Access the 'Pictures' Tool**
   - Click on the **Insert** tab in the Ribbon.
   - Choose **Pictures** to insert an image from your computer, or select **Online Pictures** to search for images online.

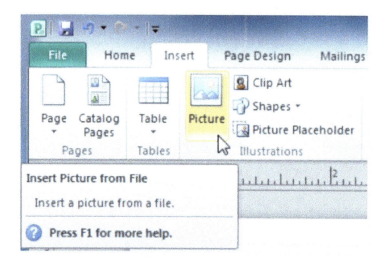

2. **Insert Your Image**

   - Browse your computer or online search results.
   - Select the image you want and click **Insert**.

3. **Resize or Rotate the Image**

   - Click the image to select it.
   - Use the corner handles to resize while maintaining proportions or the side handles to stretch the image.
   - To rotate, use the circular arrow at the top of the image.

4. **Position the Image**

   - Drag the image to place it where you want on the page.

5. **Format the Image**

   - Use the **Picture Tools Format** tab to apply effects like borders, shadows, or cropping.

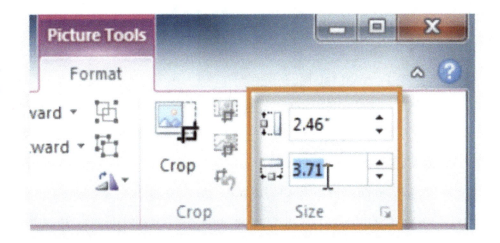

3. Adding Shapes

Shapes can highlight important sections or create visual interest. Follow these steps to add shapes:

1. **Find the 'Shapes' Tool**
   - Go to the **Insert** tab and click on **Shapes** in the Illustrations group.
2. **Choose a Shape**
   - A dropdown menu will appear with different shape options like rectangles, circles, arrows, and more.
   - Click on the shape you want to use.
3. **Draw Your Shape**
   - Your cursor will change to a crosshair.
   - Click and drag on the page to create the shape.

4. **Customize the Shape**
   - While the shape is selected, use the **Drawing Tools Format** tab to:
     - Change the shape's color.
     - Adjust the outline or add effects like shadows.
5. **Resize or Move the Shape**
   - To resize, drag the handles on the edges or corners.
   - To move, click the shape and drag it to the desired location.

Tips for Working with These Elements

- **Layering:** Right-click an element and choose **Bring to Front** or **Send to Back** to control the layering.
- **Alignment:** Use the alignment guides or tools in the **Arrange** group on the Ribbon to keep your design tidy.
- **Undo Changes:** If you make a mistake, press **Ctrl + Z** to undo.

Designing and Formatting Publications

Working with Fonts, Colors, and Page Layouts

Now that your content is in place, it's time to refine the design. Microsoft Publisher offers powerful tools for customizing fonts, colors, and page layouts to ensure your publication looks professional and visually appealing.

Working with Fonts

Fonts play a significant role in how your publication looks and feels. Here's how you can work with them effectively in Microsoft Publisher:

1. **Open Your Project**
   - Start Microsoft Publisher and open an existing file or create a new project.

2. **Select a Text Box**
   - Click on the text box where you want to change the font. If there isn't one, insert it by selecting **Insert > Draw Text Box** and clicking and dragging on your page to create it.

3. **Choose Your Font**
   - Go to the **Home** tab on the Ribbon.
   - In the **Font** group, click the dropdown menu under **Font**.
   - Browse the list of fonts and select one that matches the tone of your project.

4. **Adjust Font Size**
   - Use the font size dropdown in the same **Font** group or type in a specific size.
   - For consistent formatting, ensure headings, subheadings, and body text have appropriate size differences.

5. **Apply Font Styles**

- Use the bold, italic, or underline buttons in the **Font** group for emphasis.
- Experiment with other options like shadow, strikethrough, or all caps to enhance your design.

6. **Change Font Color**
   - Click the **Font Color** button (a colored "A" icon).
   - Select a standard color or click **More Colors** for custom options.

Working with Colors

Colors help set the mood and theme of your design. Follow these steps to incorporate colors effectively:

1. **Access the Color Options**
   - Select the element you want to colorize—this could be text, a shape, or the page background.
2. **Use Theme Colors**
   - Go to the **Page Design** tab on the Ribbon.
   - In the **Schemes** group, select a **Color Scheme** from the options available. This applies consistent colors throughout your publication.

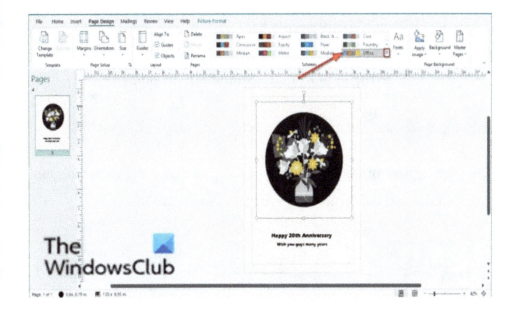

3. **Apply Specific Colors**

   - For individual elements, click **Format > Fill Color** or **Line Color** in the toolbar.

   - Choose a color or use the **Eyedropper Tool** to match a color already on your page.

4. **Create Custom Colors**

   - In the color menu, select **More Fill Colors** to create your own shade.

   - Adjust the sliders or enter specific RGB, HSL, or hex values to get precise colors.

5. **Use Gradients and Textures**
    - Add depth to your design by selecting **Gradient** or **Texture Fill** from the **Shape Fill** dropdown.

Working with Page Layouts

The page layout organizes your content and ensures everything looks professional and balanced. Here's how to customize it:

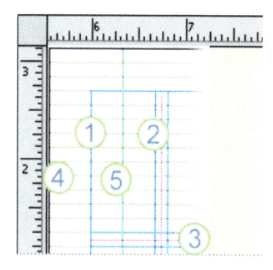

1. Margin guides

2. Column guides

3. Row guides

4. Baseline guides

5. Ruler guides

1. **Set Page Size**
    - Go to the **Page Design** tab and click **Size**.
    - Choose a standard size like A4, Letter, or Custom, depending on your needs.

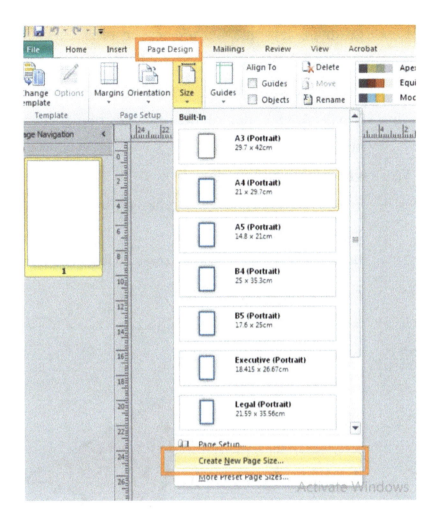

2. **Adjust Margins**

   - In the same tab, click **Margins** and select an option.
   - Use **Custom Margins** to set precise measurements.

3. **Choose a Layout Template**

   - Click **Page Design > Templates** to pick a pre-designed layout.

- Customize it to suit your project's requirements.

4. **Add and Align Elements**
   - Insert text boxes, images, or shapes via the **Insert** tab.
   - Use the **Align** options in the **Arrange** group to align items horizontally or vertically.

5. **Work with Rulers and Guides**
   - Enable rulers and guides by going to **View > Ruler** or **View > Guides**.
   - Drag guides from the rulers to create visual boundaries for precise placement.

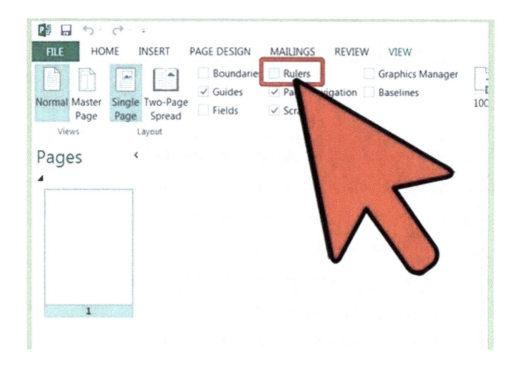

6. **Organize Layers**

- Click on any element (like an image, text box, or shape) in your design. The selection will highlight the element, showing that it's ready to be organized.

- Use the Arrange Tool to Reorganize Elements: Go to the **Home** tab in the ribbon menu. Look for the **Arrange** group. Here, you'll find options to manage layers: **Bring Forward**: Moves the selected object one layer up. **Send Backward**: Moves the selected object one layer down. **Bring to Front**: Place the selected object at the topmost layer. **Send to Back**: Sends the selected object to the bottom layer.

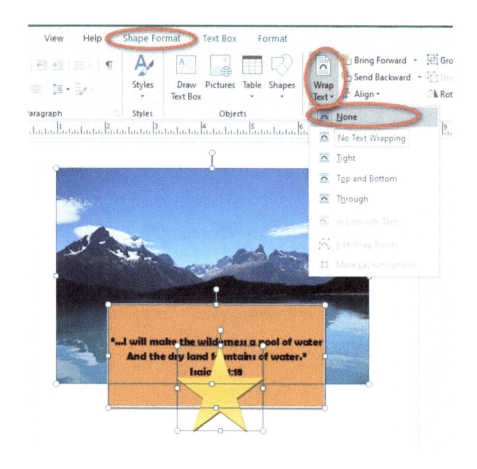

Text wrapping helps you determine how text is arranged with objects.

- Group Similar Elements Together: To make layer management easier, group related items into a single unit.
  - Select multiple objects by holding down the **Shift key** and clicking on them.
  - Right-click on the selected items, then choose **Group** from the context menu.

- Now, you can manage this group as a single layer.
- Lock Elements in Place: Prevent accidental changes by locking elements in position:
  - Select an object you want to lock.
  - Right-click and choose **Format Object** (or similar depending on the object type).
  - Look for a lock option or note the current placement to avoid unintentional adjustments.
- Use the Selection Pane for Better Organization: Go to the **Home** tab, and in the **Arrange** group, click on **Selection Pane**. The Selection Pane will list all the elements in your project. Use this pane to:
  - Rename elements for better identification.
  - Hide or show specific objects by toggling the eye icon.
  - Select elements directly without clicking on them in the design.
- Keep Layers Consistent Across Pages: If you're working on a multi-page document, ensure consistent layering:
  - Use **Master Pages** (accessible under the **View** tab) to set repeating elements, like headers or footers.
  - Apply the same layering rules to these elements to maintain uniformity.

- Preview Your Layers: Zoom out of your design to see how layers interact. Check overlapping elements to ensure everything aligns visually. Make adjustments using the Arrange tools as needed.

7. **Preview Your Layout**
   - Use the **File > Print Preview** option to see how your design will look when printed.
   - Adjust the layout if needed before finalizing.

Aligning and Positioning Elements for Professional Results

Aligning elements correctly is crucial for a polished look. Microsoft Publisher offers alignment tools that make it easy to position text boxes, images, and shapes in a balanced and organized way.

Use Guidelines for Precision

- **Enable Guides:** Click on the **View** tab and check the **Ruler Guides** and **Gridlines** options to make precise positioning easier.
- Drag and drop guides from the rulers along the top and side of the workspace. These guides act as reference lines to help you position your objects consistently.

Align Single Elements

- Select the object you want to align, such as a text box or image.
- Go to the **Arrange** group and click on the **Align** button.
- Choose an alignment option:
    - **Align Left:** Moves the object to the left edge of the page or another object.
    - **Align Center:** Centers the object horizontally or vertically.
    - **Align Right:** Moves the object to the right edge.

Align Multiple Elements

- Hold down the **Ctrl** key (Windows) or **Cmd** key (Mac) and click to select multiple objects.
- Click **Align** in the toolbar and select: **Align Top** or **Align Bottom** for vertical alignment. **Align Left**, **Align Right**, or **Center** for horizontal alignment.
- To evenly space objects, choose **Distribute Horizontally** or **Distribute Vertically.**

Grouping Objects for Unified Alignment

- Select multiple objects that should be treated as one unit.
- Right-click and choose **Group**, or use the **Group** button in the **Arrange** group.

- Align the grouped objects as you would a single item. This ensures they maintain their relative positioning.

Positioning with the Arrange Pane

- Right-click on an object and choose **Format Object**, then go to the **Position** tab.
- Use the **Position on Page** settings to manually adjust the object's coordinates.
- This method is ideal for precise adjustments and ensuring consistency across different pages.

Snap to Grid and Objects

- Enable **Snap to Grid** or **Snap to Objects** by clicking the **View** tab and selecting the respective options.
- When these features are on, your elements will automatically align to the nearest gridline or object edge, reducing manual adjustments.

Centering on the Page

- Select an object and click **Align**.
- Choose **Align Center** for horizontal centering or **Align Middle** for vertical centering.

- For perfect centering, select both options.

Layering for Depth

- Use the **Bring Forward** or **Send Backward** options in the **Arrange** group to layer objects.
- Proper layering ensures overlapping elements look organized and intentional.

Review and Refine

- Zoom in to check for alignment inconsistencies. Use the **Zoom** slider at the bottom of the workspace.
- Use the **Align to Margin Guides** feature to ensure your content stays within safe printing boundaries.
- Adjust as needed until everything looks balanced and professional.

Keyboard Shortcuts for Microsoft PowerPoint and Publisher

Keyboard Shortcuts for Microsoft PowerPoint

Keyboard shortcuts in PowerPoint help you work faster and make creating presentations smoother. Here's a categorized list of essential shortcuts:

1. General Program Controls

These shortcuts help you navigate and control the PowerPoint interface.

- **Open a new presentation:** Press Ctrl + N to create a blank presentation.
- **Save your work:** Hit Ctrl + S to save your changes immediately.
- **Open an existing presentation:** Use Ctrl + O to access a file you've already worked on.
- **Close the current presentation:** Use Ctrl + W to close it.
- **Exit PowerPoint:** Press Alt + F4 to shut down the program.

2. Navigating Slides

Make moving between slides easier with these shortcuts:

- **Move to the next slide:** Use the Page Down key.
- **Go back to the previous slide:** Hit Page Up.
- **Jump to a specific slide:** Press Ctrl + G, type the slide number, and hit Enter.

3. Editing Text and Objects

Speed up your text editing and object manipulation with these:

- **Copy:** Press Ctrl + C to duplicate selected text or objects.
- **Paste:** Use Ctrl + V to insert the copied content.
- **Cut:** Press Ctrl + X to remove selected content.
- **Undo:** If you make a mistake, press Ctrl + Z.
- **Redo:** Bring back what you've undone with Ctrl + Y.
- **Select all items on the slide:** Hit Ctrl + A.

4. Slide Formatting and Presentation Mode

Make your presentation more dynamic:

- **Start slideshow from the beginning:** Press F5.
- **Resume slideshow from the current slide:** Use Shift + F5.
- **Create a new slide:** Press Ctrl + M.
- **Duplicate a slide:** Hit Ctrl + D.
- **Switch to Slide Sorter view:** Use Alt + W + I.

5. Advanced Tips

- **Zoom in or out:** Hold Ctrl and scroll the mouse wheel.
- **Quickly align objects:** Select multiple objects and press Alt + H + A.
- **Group objects:** Use Ctrl + G to treat multiple objects as one unit.
- **Ungroup objects:** Hit Ctrl + Shift + G.

Keyboard Shortcuts for Microsoft Publisher

Microsoft Publisher is used for creating designs like brochures, flyers, and newsletters. These shortcuts will help you navigate the program like a pro:

1. General File Operations

Control your documents more effectively:

- **Create a new publication:** Press Ctrl + N.
- **Save your publication:** Use Ctrl + S.
- **Open an existing publication:** Hit Ctrl + O.
- **Print your work:** Press Ctrl + P.

2. Navigating the Workspace

Move through pages and sections:

- **Go to the next page:** Use the Page Down key.
- **Return to the previous page:** Press Page Up.
- **Switch between open publications:** Use Ctrl + F6.

3. Text and Object Management

These shortcuts are key to editing and formatting in Publisher:

- **Select all content on a page:** Press Ctrl + A.
- **Copy:** Use Ctrl + C.
- **Cut:** Press Ctrl + X.
- **Paste:** Hit Ctrl + V.
- **Bold text:** Use Ctrl + B.
- **Italicize text:** Press Ctrl + I.
- **Underline text:** Use Ctrl + U.

4. Page Design and Layout

Speed up your design process:

- **Bring object to the front:** Press Ctrl + Shift + F.
- **Send object to the back:** Use Ctrl + Shift + B.

- **Group selected objects:** Hit Ctrl + Shift + G.
- **Align selected objects:** Press Alt + J + P + A.

5. Viewing and Proofing

Make your designs look their best:

- **Zoom in or out:** Hold Ctrl and use the mouse wheel.
- **Show or hide gridlines:** Press Ctrl + Shift + F9.
- **Spellcheck:** Hit F7 to run a spellcheck.

Appendices

Appendix A: Microsoft Office 365 Tools Comparison: PowerPoint vs. Publisher

This appendix provides a detailed comparison of PowerPoint and Publisher, two key tools in the Microsoft Office 365 suite. Each tool has its strengths, and understanding their core functionalities will help you choose the right one for your specific needs. This comparison table highlights the primary functions, key features, and distinct differences between the two tools.

Tool	Primary Function	Key Features	When to Use	Key Differences
Microsoft PowerPoint	Presentation creation and editing	Slide templates, animations, transitions, multimedia integration, collaboration tools	Use for creating engaging visual presentations for meetings, events, or online sharing.	Best for dynamic, interactive presentations; not ideal for print-heavy or highly detailed publications.
Microsoft Publisher	Desktop publishing and design	Templates for brochures, newsletters, and posters, advanced layout tools, text/image integration, print optimization	Use for creating visually appealing printed materials like flyers, business cards, or menus.	Best for static, print-focused content; lacks multimedia features like animations and transitions.

Appendix B: Troubleshooting Common Issues in Microsoft PowerPoint and Publisher

This section provides solutions to common problems users may encounter while working with PowerPoint and Publisher. By following these troubleshooting steps, you can quickly resolve issues and maintain productivity.

Troubleshooting Common Issues in Microsoft PowerPoint

1. **Problem: PowerPoint Crashes When Adding Media**
   Cause: Corrupted media files or outdated software.
   Solution:
   - Ensure your media files (e.g., videos or audio) are in supported formats like .MP4 or .MP3.
   - Update PowerPoint by going to *File > Account > Update Options > Update Now.*

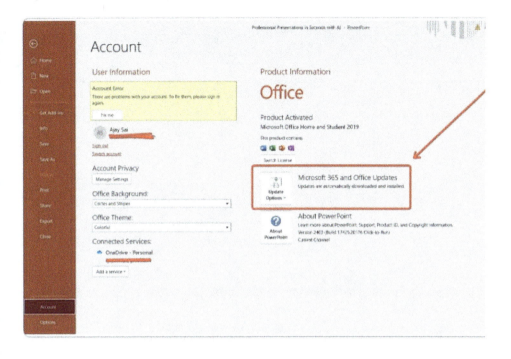

- Reduce the file size of large media files.
- Disable add-ins:
    - Go to *File > Options > Add-ins*.
    - Under Manage, select *COM Add-ins*, and click *Go*.
    - Uncheck unnecessary add-ins and restart PowerPoint.

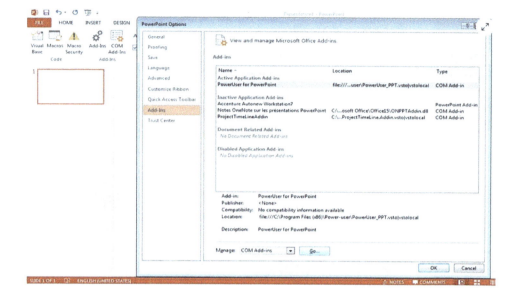

2. **Problem: Animations Not Playing Properly**

   Cause: Incompatible file formats or unsupported transitions.

   Solution:

   - Check the animation settings under *Animations > Animation Pane*.

   - Ensure that animations are compatible with the version of PowerPoint you're using.

   - If sharing a presentation, save it as a PowerPoint Show (.ppsx) to preserve animations.

3. **Problem: PowerPoint Slides Appear Blurry**

   Cause: Low-resolution images or display settings.

   Solution:

   - Use high-resolution images (300 DPI or higher).

- Adjust slide size for optimal display: *Design > Slide Size > Custom Slide Size.*

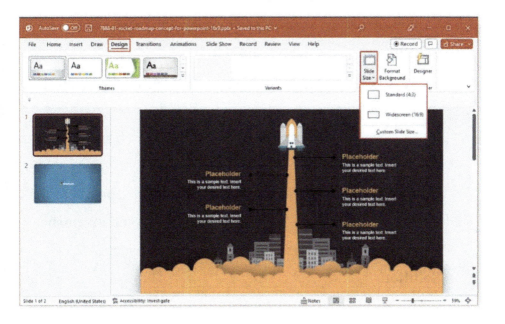

- Check display settings in your operating system to ensure they match your screen's resolution.

4. **Problem: Presentation Not Displaying Correctly on Another Device**

   Cause: Missing fonts or unsupported formats.

   Solution:
   - Embed fonts: *File > Options > Save > Embed fonts in the file.*
   - Save the presentation as a PDF for consistent formatting.

Troubleshooting Common Issues in Microsoft Publisher

1. **Problem: Publisher Files Look Different When Printed**

   Cause: Printer settings or incompatible formats.

   Solution:

   - Use the *Print Preview* feature to check alignment before printing.
   - Ensure your printer supports the paper size and layout used.
   - Convert your publication to a PDF: *File > Save As > PDF*.

2. **Problem: Images Are Missing or Not Displayed Properly**

   Cause: Missing linked files or unsupported formats.

   Solution:

   - Re-link missing images: *File > Info > Manage Embedded Files*.
   - Use supported image formats like .PNG or .JPEG.

3. **Problem: Publisher Keeps Crashing**

   Cause: Corrupted templates or add-ins.

   Solution:

   - Delete or rename corrupted templates:
     - Navigate to *C:\Users[YourUsername]\AppData\Roaming\Microsoft\Templates*.

- Rename the template file (e.g., Normal.pub to Normal_old.pub).
- Disable add-ins through *File > Options > Add-ins*.

4. **Problem: Text Overflow in Publications**

   Cause: Text boxes too small for content.

   Solution:
   - Use the *Text Fit* option under the *Format* tab to resize text automatically.

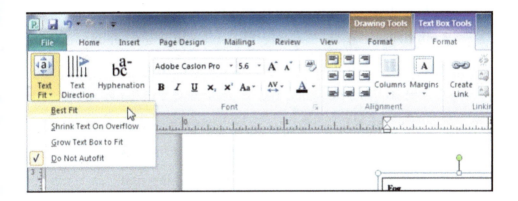

   - Expand text boxes manually or link text boxes to flow text across multiple areas.

Appendix C: Glossary of Key Terms

This glossary provides definitions of essential terms used in the context of PowerPoint and Publisher, reinforcing your understanding of these tools.

- **Slide Layout:** Pre-designed arrangements of content placeholders on PowerPoint slides.
- **Master Slide:** A template in PowerPoint that controls the design and layout of all slides in a presentation.
- **Animation Pane:** A feature in PowerPoint that allows users to manage the sequence and timing of animations on a slide.
- **Template:** Pre-designed file structures in Publisher for creating documents such as brochures, newsletters, and posters.
- **Text Overflow:** Occurs in Publisher when there is more text than a text box can display, indicated by a red plus sign.
- **Print Bleed:** A margin outside the design area in Publisher, ensuring that printed designs extend to the edge of the paper without borders.

Index

www.ingramcontent.com/pod-product-compliance
Lightning Source LLC
LaVergne TN
LVHW052055060326
832903LV00061B/975